YES YOU CAN SERIES

MARIA D' ANDREA'S

BOOK OF
COMMON
PRAYER

An Administration Of The Sacraments And Other Rites Adapted By The House Of Enlightenment

Maria D' Andrea

YES YOU CAN SERIES

Maria D'Andrea's

Book of

Common Prayer

An Administration of the Sacraments and Other Rites

Adapted by the "House of Enlightenment"

INNER LIGHT/GLOBAL COMMUNICATIONS

YES YOU CAN SERIES

Maria D'Andrea's Book of Common Prayer

By Maria D'Andrea, MsD, D.D., DRH

© 2017 Maria D'Andrea

Published by Timothy Green Beckley

DBA Inner Light/Global Communications - All Rights Reserved

Printed in the United States of America

Non-Fiction

Timothy Green Beckley: Editorial Director

Carol Ann Rodriguez: Publishers Assistant

Editor/Layout & Graphics: Tim R. Swartz

Sean Casteel: Associate Editor

William Kern: Associate Editor

Email: mrufo8@hotmail.com

www.ConspiracyJournal.Com

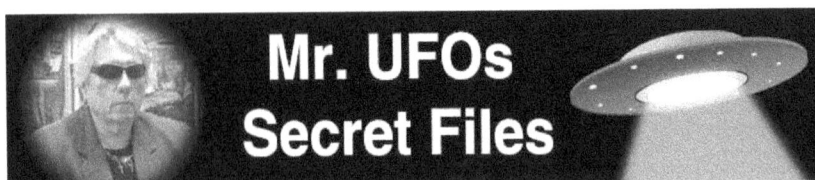

https://www.youtube.com/user/MRUFO1100

CONTENTS

DEDICATION

To my sons: Rick Holecek and Rob D'Andrea

Both are ministers, who are positive in helping others to find their right paths for happiness and to guide them in times of trouble and stress.

They give guidance in all areas of life to empower others to make better choices so they can attain a better life.

They also perform ceremonies for all occasions.

ABOUT US

*T*he House of Enlightenment was founded by Rev. Maria D'Andrea. We are a Spiritual Interfaith Ministry. We feel there is One Source and whichever Path you choose to take there is the one that is right for you.

We ONLY do positive and believe in not harming anyone.

We share our knowledge with others. Esoteric discussions should be an adventure, interesting and not trying to change another's point of view. We are all short of absolute, full knowledge or we would not be in the physical body.

We are always growing and expanding as children of God /Our Source.

We do not promote only one religion / belief system. We are all connected spiritually. As in the spider web: think of it as if you have each soul / spirit on this plane of existence somewhere on a strand and when one soul shakes the web, it shakes everyone.

We are truly all connected.

The following are services to give you a base to work from. You may read just them or come up with your own. You may have a couple who writes their own vows, request that you write one specifically for them, do a commitment ceremony or a ritual / ceremony that they feel expresses who they are.

There isn't only one way to be of service to others. Do what you feel is the best for each individual or situation.

Go forth and be of service.

Rev. Maria D'Andrea MsD, D.D., DRH, DPR

"The First Amendment (Amendment I) to the United States Constitution prohibits the making of any law respecting an establishment of religion, impeding the free exercise of religion, abridging the freedom of speech, infringing on the freedom of the press, interfering with the right to peaceably assemble."

PRAYERS

The Lords Prayer

The people stand or kneel

Officiate The Lord be with you.

People And with thy spirit.

Officiate Let us pray.

Officiate and People

Our Father, who art in heaven,

hallowed be thy Name,

thy kingdom come,

thy will be done,

on earth as it is in heaven.

Give us this day our daily bread.

And forgive us our trespasses,

as we forgive those who trespass against us.

And lead us not into temptation,

but deliver us from evil.

For thine is the kingdom, and the power, and the glory,

for ever and ever. Amen.

The Apostles' Creed

Officiante and People together, all standing

I believe in God, the Father almighty,

maker of heaven and earth;

And in Jesus Christ his only Son our Lord;

who was conceived by the Holy Ghost,

born of the Virgin Mary,

suffered under Pontius Pilate,

was crucified, dead, and buried.

He descended into hell.

Morning Prayer I 53

The third day he rose again from the dead.

He ascended into heaven,

and sitteth on the right hand of God the Father almighty.

From thence he shall come to judge the quick and the dead.

I believe in the Holy Ghost,

the holy catholic Church,

the communion of saints,

the forgiveness of sins,

the resurrection of the body,

and the life everlasting. Amen.

<u>The General Thanksgiving</u>

Officiate and People

Almighty God, Father of all mercies,

we thine unworthy servants

do give thee most humble and hearty thanks

for all thy goodness and loving-kindness

to us and to all men.

We bless thee for our creation, preservation,

and all the blessings of this life;

but above all for thine inestimable love

in the redemption of the world by our Lord Jesus Christ,

for the means of grace, and for the hope of glory.

<u>Non- Denominational Prayer</u>

By Rev. Maria D'Andrea

May Divine Power (<u>you may replace Divine Power with the term you are most comfortable with</u>) bless us and keep us safe.

May we always be protected.

May we be Divinely guided to make the right choices in our lives.

May we be of service to others.

May we help those less fortunate then us.

May we be loving and loved.

May we open our hearts and live in Your Light.

AN ORDER OF SERVICE

Officiate O God, make speed to save us.

People O Lord, make haste to help us.

Officiate and People

Glory to the Father, and to the Son, and to the Holy Spirit: as

it was in the beginning, is now, and will be for ever. Amen.

Except in Lent, add Alleluia. A suitable hymn may be sung. One or more of the following Psalms is sung or said. Other suitable selections include Psalms 19, 67; one or more sections of Psalm 119, or a selection from Psalms 120 through 133.

107 I am deeply troubled; preserve my life, O Lord, according to your word.

108 Accept, O Lord, the willing tribute of my lips, and teach me your judgments.

109 My life is always in my hand, yet I do not forget your law.

110 The wicked have set a trap for me, but I have not strayed from your commandments.

111 Your decrees are my inheritance for ever; truly, they are the joy of my heart.

112 I have applied my heart to fulfill your statutes for ever and to the end.

<u>Psalm 121</u>

1. I lift up my eyes to the hills; from where is my help to come?

2. My help comes from the LORD, the maker of heaven and earth.

3. He will not let your foot be moved and he who watches over you will not fall asleep.

4. Behold, he who keeps watch over Israel shall neither slumber nor sleep;

5. The Lord himself watches over you; the Lord is your shade at your right hand,

6. So that the sun shall not strike you by day, nor the moon by night.

7. The Lord shall preserve you from all evil; it is he who shall keep you safe.

8. The Lord shall watch over your going out and your coming in, from this time forth for evermore.

Psalm 126

1. When the Lord restored the fortunes of Zion, then were we like those who dream.

2. Then was our mouth filled with laughter, and our tongue with shouts of joy.

3. Then they said among the nations, "The Lord has done great things for them."

4. The Lord has done great things for us, and we are glad indeed.

5. Restore our fortunes, O Lord, like the watercourses of the Negev.

6. Those who sowed with tears will reap with songs of joy.

7. Those who go out weeping, carrying the seed, will come again with joy, shouldering their sheaves.

At the end of the Psalms is sung or said.

Glory to the Father, and to the Son, and to the Holy Spirit: as it was in the beginning, is now, and will be for ever. Amen.

One of the following, or some other suitable passage of Scripture, is read.

The love of God has been poured into our hearts through the Holy Spirit that has been given to us. Romans 5:5

People: *Thanks be to God, or the following.*

If anyone is in Christ he is a new creation; the old has passed away, behold the new has come. All this is from God, who through Christ reconciled us to himself and gave us the ministry of reconciliation. 2 Corinthians 5:17-18

People: *Thanks be to God, or this.*

From the rising of the sun to its setting my Name shall be great among the nations, and in every place incense shall be offered to my Name, and a pure offering; for my Name shall be great among the nations, says the Lord of Hosts. Malachi 1:11

People Thanks be to God.

A meditation, silent or spoken, may follow.

Silence may be kept after each Reading. One of the following Canticles, or sung or said after each Reading. If three Lessons are used, the Lesson from the Gospel is read after the second Canticle.

1 A Song of Creation

Song of the Three Young Men, this Canticle may be shortened by omitting section II or III.

I Invocation

O all ye works of the Lord, bless ye the Lord;

praise him and magnify him for ever.

O ye angels of the Lord, bless ye the Lord;

praise him and magnify him for ever.

II The Cosmic Order

O ye heavens, bless ye the Lord;

O ye waters that be above the firmament, bless ye the Lord;

O all ye powers of the Lord, bless ye the Lord;

praise him and magnify him for ever.

O ye sun and moon, bless ye the Lord;

O ye stars of heaven, bless ye the Lord;

O ye showers and dew, bless ye the Lord;

praise him and magnify him for ever.

O ye winds of God, bless ye the Lord;

O ye fire and heat, bless ye the Lord;

O ye winter and summer, bless ye the Lord;

praise him and magnify him for ever.

O ye dews and frosts, bless ye the Lord;

O ye frost and cold, bless ye the Lord;

O ye ice and snow, bless ye the Lord;

praise him and magnify him for ever.

O ye nights and days, bless ye the Lord;

O ye light and darkness, bless ye the Lord;

O ye lightnings and clouds, bless ye the Lord;

praise him and magnify him for ever.

III The Earth and its Creatures

O let the earth bless the Lord;

O ye mountains and hills, bless ye the Lord;

O all ye green things upon the earth, bless ye the Lord;

praise him and magnify him for ever.

O ye wells, bless ye the Lord;

O ye seas and floods, bless ye the Lord;

O ye whales and all that move in the waters, bless ye the Lord;

praise him and magnify him for ever.

O all ye fowls of the air, bless ye the Lord;

O all ye beasts and cattle, bless ye the Lord;

O ye children of men, bless ye the Lord;

praise him and magnify him for ever.

IV The People of God

O ye people of God, bless ye the Lord;
O ye priests of the Lord, bless ye the Lord;
O ye servants of the Lord, bless ye the Lord;
praise him and magnify him for ever.
O ye spirits and souls of the righteous, bless ye the Lord;
O ye holy and humble men of heart, bless ye the Lord.
Let us bless the Father, the Son, and the Holy Spirit;
praise him and magnify him for ever.

2 A Song of Praise

Song of the Three Young Men,

Blessed art thou, O Lord God of our fathers;

praised and exalted above all for ever.

Blessed art thou for the Name of thy Majesty;

praised and exalted above all for ever.

Blessed art thou in the temple of thy holiness;

praised and exalted above all for ever.

Blessed art thou that beholdest the depths,

and dwellest between the Cherubim;

praised and exalted above all for ever.

Blessed art thou on the glorious throne of thy kingdom;

praised and exalted above all for ever.

Blessed art thou in the firmament of heaven;

praised and exalted above all for ever.

Blessed art thou, O Father, Son, and Holy Spirit;

praised and exalted above all for ever.

3 The Song of Mary

Luke 1:46-55
My soul doth magnify the Lord,
and my spirit hath rejoiced in God my Savior.
For he hath regarded
the lowliness of his handmaiden.
For behold from henceforth
all generations shall call me blessed.

For he that is mighty hath magnified me,

and holy is his Name.

And his mercy is on them that fear him

throughout all generations.

He hath showed strength with his arm;

he hath scattered the proud in the imagination of their hearts.

He hath put down the mighty from their seat,

and hath exalted the humble and meek.

He hath filled the hungry with good things,

and the rich he hath sent empty away.

He remembering his mercy hath holpen his servant Israel,

as he promised to our forefathers,

Abraham and his seed for ever.

Glory to the Father, and to the Son, and to the Holy Spirit:

as it was in the beginning, is now, and will be for ever. Amen.

4 The Song of Zechariah

Luke 1:68-79

Blessed be the Lord God of Israel,

for he hath visited and redeemed his people;

And hath raised up a mighty salvation for us

in the house of his servant David,

As he spake by the mouth of his holy prophets,

which have been since the world began:

That we should be saved from our enemies,

and from the hand of all that hate us;

To perform the mercy promised to our forefathers,

and to remember his holy covenant;

To perform the oath which he sware to our forefather Abraham,

that he would give us,

That we being delivered out of the hand of our enemies

might serve him without fear,

In holiness and righteousness before him,

all the days of our life.

And thou, child, shalt be called the prophet of the Highest,

for thou shalt go before the face of the Lord

to prepare his ways;

To give knowledge of salvation unto his people

for the remission of their sins,

Through the tender mercy of our God,

whereby the dayspring from on high hath visited us;

To give light to them that sit in darkness

and in the shadow of death,

and to guide our feet into the way of peace

Glory to the Father, and to the Son, and to the Holy Spirit:

as it was in the beginning, is now, and will be for ever. Amen.

5 The Song of Simeon

Luke 2:29-32

Lord, now lettest thou thy servant depart in peace,

according to thy word;

For mine eyes have seen thy salvation,

which thou hast prepared before the face of all people,

To be a light to lighten the Gentiles,

and to be the glory of thy people Israel.

Glory to the Father, and to the Son, and to the Holy Spirit:

as it was in the beginning, is now, and will be for ever. Amen.

6 Glory be to God

Glory be to God on high,

and on earth peace, good will towards men.

We praise thee, we bless thee,

we worship thee,

we glorify thee,

we give thanks to thee for thy great glory,

O Lord God, heavenly King, God the Father Almighty.

O Lord, the only-begotten Son, Jesus Christ;

O Lord God, Lamb of God, Son of the Father,

that takest away the sins of the world,

have mercy upon us.

Thou that takest away the sins of the world,

receive our prayer.

Thou that sittest at the right hand of God the Father,

have mercy upon us.

For thou only art holy,

thou only art the Lord,

thou only, O Christ,

with the Holy Ghost,

art most high in the glory of God the Father. Amen.

7 We Praise Thee

We praise thee, O God; we acknowledge thee to be the Lord.

All the earth doth worship thee, the Father everlasting.

To thee all Angels cry aloud,

the Heavens and all the Powers therein.

To thee Cherubim and Seraphim continually do cry:

Holy, holy, holy, Lord God of Sabaoth;

Heaven and earth are full of the majesty of thy glory.

The glorious company of the apostles praise thee.

The goodly fellowship of the prophets praise thee.

The noble army of martyrs praise thee.

The holy Church throughout all the world

doth acknowledge thee,

the Father, of an infinite majesty,

thine adorable, true, and only Son,

also the Holy Ghost the Comforter.

Thou art the King of glory, O Christ.

Thou art the everlasting Son of the Father.

When thou tookest upon thee to deliver man,

thou didst humble thyself to be born of a Virgin.

When thou hadst overcome the sharpness of death,

thou didst open the kingdom of heaven to all believers.

Thou sittest at the right hand of God, in the glory of the Father.

We believe that thou shalt come to be our judge.

We therefore pray thee, help thy servants,

whom thou hast redeemed with thy precious blood.

Make them to be numbered with thy saints,

in glory everlasting.

The Lessons

One or two Lessons, as appointed, are read, the Reader first saying

A Reading (Lesson) from _____.

A citation giving chapter and verse may be added. After each Lesson the Reader may say The Word of the Lord.

Answer: Thanks be to God.

Silence may be kept after each Reading. One of the following Canticles, or sung or said after each Reading. If three Lessons are used, the Lesson from the Gospel is read after the second Canticle.

8 The Song of Moses

Exodus 15:1-6, 11-13, 17-18

Especially suitable for use in Easter Season.

I will sing to the Lord, for he is lofty and uplifted;

the horse and its rider has he hurled into the sea.

The Lord is my strength and my refuge;

the Lord has become my Savior.

This is my God and I will praise him,

the God of my people and I will exalt him.

The Lord is a mighty warrior;

Yahweh is his Name.

The chariots of Pharaoh and his army has he hurled into the sea;

the finest of those who bear armor have been

drowned in the Red Sea.

The fathomless deep has overwhelmed them;

they sank into the depths like a stone.

Your right hand, O Lord, is glorious in might;

your right hand, O Lord, has overthrown the enemy.

Who can be compared with you, O Lord, among the gods?

who is like you, glorious in holiness,

awesome in renown, and worker of wonders?

You stretched forth your right hand;

the earth swallowed them up.

With your constant love you led the people you redeemed;

with your might you brought them in safety to

your holy dwelling.

You will bring them in and plant them

on the mount of your possession,

The resting-place you have made for yourself, O Lord,

the sanctuary, O Lord, that your hand has established.

The Lord shall reign *

for ever and for ever.

Glory to the Father, and to the Son, and to the Holy Spirit:

as it was in the beginning, is now, and will be for ever. Amen.

9 The First Song of Isaiah

Isaiah 12:2-6

Surely, it is God who saves me;

I will trust in him and not be afraid.

For the Lord is my stronghold and my sure defense,

and he will be my Savior.

Therefore you shall draw water with rejoicing

from the springs of salvation.

And on that day you shall say,

Give thanks to the Lord and call upon his Name;

Make his deeds known among the peoples;

see that they remember that his Name is exalted.

Sing the praises of the Lord, for he has done great things,

and this is known in all the world.

Cry aloud, inhabitants of Zion, ring out your joy,

for the great one in the midst of you is the Holy One of Israel.

Glory to the Father, and to the Son, and to the Holy Spirit:

as it was in the beginning, is now, and will be for ever. Amen.

10 The Second Song of Isaiah

Isaiah 55:6-11

Seek the Lord while he wills to be found;

call upon him when he draws near.

Let the wicked forsake their ways

and the evil ones their thoughts;

And let them turn to the Lord, and he will have compassion,

and to our God, for he will richly pardon.

For my thoughts are not your thoughts,

nor your ways my ways, says the Lord.

For as the heavens are higher than the earth,

so are my ways higher than your ways,

and my thoughts than your thoughts.

For as rain and snow fall from the heavens

and return not again, but water the earth,

Bringing forth life and giving growth,

seed for sowing and bread for eating,

So is my word that goes forth from my mouth;

it will not return to me empty;

But it will accomplish that which I have purposed,

and prosper in that for which I sent it.

Glory to the Father, and to the Son, and to the Holy Spirit:

as it was in the beginning, is now, and will be for ever. Amen.

11 The Third Song of Isaiah Surge

Isaiah 60:1-3, 11a, 14c, 18-19

Arise, shine, for your light has come,

and the glory of the Lord has dawned upon you.

For behold, darkness covers the land;

deep gloom enshrouds the peoples.

But over you the Lord will rise,

and his glory will appear upon you.

Nations Will stream to your light,

and kings to the brightness of your dawning.

Your gates will always be open;

by day or night they will never be shut.

They will call you, The City of the Lord,

The Zion of the Holy One of Israel.

Violence will no more be heard in your land,

ruin or destruction within your borders.

You will call your walls, Salvation,

and all your portals, Praise.

The sun will no more be your light by day;

by night you will not need the brightness of the moon.

The Lord will be your everlasting light,

and your God will be your glory.

Glory to the Father, and to the Son, and to the Holy Spirit:

as it was in the beginning, is now and ever shall be. Amen.

I The Cosmic Order

Glorify the Lord, you angels and all powers of the Lord,

O heavens and all waters above the heavens.

Sun and moon and stars of the sky, glorify the Lord,

praise him and highly exalt him for ever.

Glorify the Lord, every shower of rain and fall of dew,

all winds and fire and heat.

Winter and summer, glorify the Lord,

praise him and highly exalt him for ever.

Glorify the Lord, O chill and cold,

drops of dew and flakes of snow.

Frost and cold, ice and sleet, glorify the Lord,

praise him and highly exalt him for ever.

Glorify the Lord, O nights and days,

O shining light and enfolding dark.

Storm clouds and thunderbolts, glorify the Lord,

praise him and highly exalt him for ever.

II The Earth and its Creatures

Let the earth glorify the Lord,

praise him and highly exalt him for ever.

Glorify the Lord, O mountains and hills,

and all that grows upon the earth,

praise him and highly exalt him for ever.

Glorify the Lord, O springs of water, seas, and streams,

O whales and all that move in the waters.

All birds of the air, glorify the Lord,

praise him and highly exalt him for ever.

Glorify the Lord, O beasts of the wild,

and all you flocks and herds.

O men and women everywhere, glorify the Lord,

praise him and highly exalt him for ever.

III The People of God

Let the people of God glorify the Lord,

praise him and highly exalt him for ever.

Glorify the Lord, O priests and servants of the Lord,

praise him and highly exalt him for ever.

Glorify the Lord, O spirits and souls of the righteous,

praise him and highly exalt him for ever.

You that are holy and humble of heart, glorify the Lord,

praise him and highly exalt him for ever.

Doxology

Let us glorify the Lord: Father, Son, and Holy Spirit;

praise him and highly exalt him for ever.

In the firmament of his power, glorify the Lord,

praise him and highly exalt him for ever.

13 A Song of Three Young Men

Glory to you, Lord God of our fathers;

you are worthy of praise; glory to you.

Glory to you for the radiance of your holy Name;

we will praise you and highly exalt you for ever.

Glory to you in the splendor of your temple;

on the throne of your majesty, glory to you.

Glory to you, seated between the Cherubim;

we will praise you and highly exalt you for ever.

Glory to you, beholding the depths;

in the high vault of heaven, glory to you.

Glory to you, Father, Son, and Holy Spirit;

we will praise you and highly exalt you for ever.

14 A Song of Penitence

Prayer of Manasseh, 1-2, 4, 6-7, 11-15

Especially suitable in Lent, and on other penitential occasions

O Lord and Ruler of the hosts of heaven,

God of Abraham, Isaac, and Jacob,

and of all their righteous offspring:

You made the heavens and the earth,

with all their vast array.

All things quake with fear at your presence;

they tremble because of your power.

But your merciful promise is beyond all measure;

it surpasses all that our minds can fathom.

O Lord, you are full of compassion,

long-suffering, and abounding in mercy.

You hold back your hand;

you do not punish as we deserve.

In your great goodness, Lord,

you have promised forgiveness to sinners,

that they may repent of their sin and be saved.

And now, O Lord, I bend the knee of my heart,

and make my appeal, sure of your gracious goodness.

I have sinned, O Lord, I have sinned,

and I know my wickedness only too well.

Therefore I make this prayer to you:

Forgive me, Lord, forgive me.

Do not let me perish in my sin,

nor condemn me to the depths of the earth.

For you, O Lord, are the God of those who repent,

and in me you will show forth your goodness.

Unworthy as I am, you will save me,

in accordance with your great mercy,

and I will praise you without ceasing all the days of my life.

For all the powers of heaven sing your praises,

and yours is the glory to ages of ages. Amen.

15 The Song of Mary

Luke 1:46-55

My soul proclaims the greatness of the Lord,

my spirit rejoices in God my Savior;

for he has looked with favor on his lowly servant.

From this day all generations will call me blessed:

the Almighty has done great things for me,

and holy is his Name.

He has mercy on those who fear him

in every generation.

He has shown the strength of his arm,

he has scattered the proud in their conceit.

He has cast down the mighty from their thrones,

and has lifted up the lowly.

He has filled the hungry with good things,

and the rich he has sent away empty.

He has come to the help of his servant Israel,

for he has remembered his promise of mercy,

The promise he made to our fathers,

to Abraham and his children for ever.

Glory to the Father, and to the Son, and to the Holy Spirit:

as it was in the beginning, is now, and will be for ever. Amen.

16 The Song of Zechariah

Luke 1:68-79

Blessed be the Lord, the God of Israel;

he has come to his people and set them free.

He has raised up for us a mighty savior,

born of the house of his servant David.

Through his holy prophets he promised of old,

that he would save us from our enemies,

from the hands of all who hate us.

He promised to show mercy to our fathers

and to remember his holy covenant.

This was the oath he swore to our father Abraham,

to set us free from the hands of our enemies,

Free to worship him without fear,

holy and righteous in his sight

all the days of our life.

You, my child, shall be called the prophet of the Most High,

for you will go before the Lord to prepare his way,

To give his people knowledge of salvation

by the forgiveness of their sins.

In the tender compassion of our God

the dawn from on high shall break upon us,

To shine on those who dwell in darkness and the

shadow of death,

and to guide our feet into the way of peace.

Glory to the Father, and to the Son, and to the Holy Spirit:

as it was in the beginning, is now, and will be for ever. Amen.

17 The Song of Simeon

Luke 2:29-32
Lord, you now have set your servant free
to go in peace as you have promised;
For these eyes of mine have seen the Savior,
whom you have prepared for all the world to see:
A Light to enlighten the nations,
and the glory of your people Israel.
Glory to the Father, and to the Son, and to the Holy Spirit:

as it was in the beginning, is now, and will be for ever. Amen.

18 A Song to the Lamb

Revelation 4:11; 5:9-10, 13

Splendor and honor and kingly power

are yours by right, O Lord our God,

For you created everything that is,

and by your will they were created and have their being;

And yours by right, O Lamb that was slain,

for with your blood you have redeemed for God,

From every family, language, people, and nation,

a kingdom of priests to serve our God.

And so, to him who sits upon the throne,

and to Christ the Lam

Be worship and praise, dominion and splendor,

for ever and for evermore.

19 The Song of the Redeemed

Revelation 15:3-4

O ruler of the universe, Lord God,

great deeds are they that you have done,

surpassing human understanding.

Your ways are ways of righteousness and truth,

O King of all the ages.

Who can fail to do you homage, Lord,

and sing the praises of your Name?

for you only are the holy One.

All nations will draw near and fall down before you,

because your just and holy works have been revealed.

Glory to the Father, and to the Son, and to the Holy Spirit:

as it was in the beginning, is now, and will be for ever. Amen.

20 Glory to God

Glory to God in the highest,

and peace to his people on earth.

Lord God, heavenly King,

almighty God and Father,

we worship you, we give you thanks,

we praise you for your glory.

Lord Jesus Christ, only Son of the Father,

Lord God, Lamb of God,

you take away the sin of the world;

have mercy on us;

you are seated at the right hand of the Father;

receive our prayer.

For you alone are the Holy One,

you alone are the Lord,

you alone are the Most High,

Jesus Christ,

with the Holy Spirit,

in the glory of the Father.

PASTORAL OFFICES

Concerning the Service

In the Daily Office, the term "Officiate" is used to denote the person, clerical or lay, who leads the Office, Service or Ceremony. Such as marriage, baptism / name giving, funeral or other religious service. Officiate / priest / minister, other religious clergy are usually ordained by a religious denomination as members of the clergy.

Various Occasions

For optional use, when desired, subject to the rules set forth in the Calendar of the Church Year.

1. Of the Holy Trinity

Almighty God, who hast revealed to thy Church thine eternal

Being of glorious majesty and perfect love as one God in

Trinity of Persons: Give us grace to continue steadfast in the

confession of this faith, and constant in our worship of thee,

Father, Son, and Holy Spirit; who livest and reignest, one

God, now and for ever. Amen.

Preface of Trinity Sunday

2. Of the Holy Spirit

Almighty and most merciful God, grant, we beseech thee,

that by the indwelling of thy Holy Spirit we may be enlightened and strengthened for thy service; through Jesus Christ our Lord, who liveth and reigneth with thee, in the unity of the same Spirit ever, one God, world without end. Amen.

Preface of Pentecost

3. Of the Holy Angels

O everlasting God, who hast ordained and constituted the ministries of angels and men in a wonderful order: Mercifully grant that, as thy holy angels always serve and worship thee in heaven, so by thy appointment they may help and defend us on earth; through Jesus Christ our Lord, who liveth and reigneth with thee and the Holy Spirit, one God, for ever and ever. Amen.

Preface of Trinity Sunday

4. Of the Incarnation

O God, who didst wonderfully create, and yet more wonderfully restore, the dignity of human nature: Grant that we may share the divine life of him who humbled himself to share our humanity, thy Son Jesus Christ; who liveth and reigneth with thee, in the unity of the Holy Spirit, one God, for ever and ever. Amen.

Preface of the Epiphany

5. Of the Holy Eucharist

Especially suitable for Thursdays

God our Father, whose Son our Lord Jesus Christ in a wonderful Sacrament hath left unto us a memorial of his passion: Grant us so to venerate the sacred mysteries of his Body and Blood, that we may ever perceive within ourselves the fruit of his redemption; who liveth and reigneth with thee and the Holy Spirit, one God, for ever and ever. Amen.

Preface of the Epiphany

6. Of the Holy Cross

Especially suitable for Fridays

Almighty God, whose beloved Son willingly endured the agony and shame of the cross for our redemption: Give us courage, we beseech thee, to take up our cross and follow him; who liveth and reigneth with thee and the Holy Spirit, one God, now and for ever. Amen.

Preface of Holy Week

7. For All Baptized Christians

Especially suitable for Saturdays

Grant, O Lord God, to all who have been baptized into the death and resurrection of thy Son Jesus Christ, that, as we have put away the old life of sin, so we may be renewed in the spirit of our minds, and live in righteousness and true holiness; through the same Jesus Christ our Lord, who liveth and reigneth with thee, in the unity of the Holy Spirit, one God, now and for ever. Amen.

Preface of Baptism

8. For the Departed

O eternal Lord God, who holdest all souls in life: Give, we beseech thee, to thy whole Church in paradise and on earth thy light and thy peace; and grant that we, following the good examples of those who have served thee here and are now at rest, may at the last enter with them into thine unending joy; through Jesus Christ our Lord, who liveth and reigneth with thee, in the unity of the Holy Spirit, one God, now and for ever. Amen.

Or this...

Almighty God, we remember this day before thee thy faithful servant N.; and we pray that, having opened to him the gates *of larger life, thou wilt receive him more and more into thy*

joyful service, that, with all who have faithfully served thee in

the past, he may share in the eternal victory of Jesus Christ

our Lord; who liveth and reigneth with thee, in the unity of

the Holy Spirit, one God, for ever and ever. Amen.

Any of the Collects appointed for use at the Burial of the Dead may be used instead. For the Prayers of the People, one of the forms appointed for the Burial of the Dead may be used.

9. Of the Reign of Christ

Almighty and everlasting God, whose will it is to restore all

things in thy well-beloved Son, the King of kings and Lord of

lords: Mercifully grant that the peoples of the earth, divided

and enslaved by sin, may be freed and brought together

under his most gracious rule; who liveth and reigneth with

thee and the Holy Spirit, one God, now and for ever. Amen.

Preface of the Ascension, or of Baptism

10. At Baptism

Almighty God, who by our baptism into the death and

resurrection of thy Son Jesus Christ dost turn us from the old

life of sin: Grant that we, being reborn to new life in him, may live in righteousness and holiness all our days; through the same thy Son Jesus Christ our Lord, who liveth and reigneth with thee and the Holy Spirit, one God, now and for ever. Amen.

Preface of Baptism

11. At Confirmation

Grant, Almighty God, that we, who have been redeemed from the old life of sin by our baptism into the death and resurrection of thy Son Jesus Christ, may be renewed in thy Holy Spirit, and live in righteousness and true holiness; through the same Jesus Christ our Lord, who liveth and reigneth with thee and the same Spirit, one God, now and for ever. Amen.

Preface of Baptism, or of Pentecost

12. On the Anniversary of the Dedication of a Church

O Almighty God, to whose glory we celebrate the dedication of this house of prayer: We give thee thanks for the fellowship of those who have worshiped in this place; and we pray that all who seek thee here may find thee, and be filled with thy joy and peace; through Jesus Christ our Lord, who liveth and reigneth with thee, in the unity of the Holy Spirit, one God, now and for ever. Amen.

13. For a Church Convention

Almighty and everlasting Father, who hast given the Holy Spirit to abide with us for ever: Bless, we beseech thee, with his grace and presence, the bishops and the other clergy and the laity here (or now, or soon to be) assembled in thy Name, that thy Church, being preserved in true faith and godly discipline, may fulfill all the mind of him who loved it and gave himself for it, thy Son Jesus Christ our Savior; who liveth and reigneth with thee, in the unity of the same Spirit, one God, now and for ever. Amen.

Preface of Pentecost, or of the Season

14. For the Unity of the Church

Almighty Father, whose blessed Son before his passion prayed for his disciples that they might be one, even as thou and he are one: Grant that thy Church, being bound together in love and obedience to thee, may be united in one body by the one Spirit, that the world may believe in him whom thou didst send, the same thy Son Jesus Christ our Lord; who liveth and reigneth with thee, in the unity of the same Spirit, one God, now and for ever. Amen.

Preface of Baptism, or of Trinity Sunday

15. For the Ministry (Ember Days)

For use on the traditional days or at other times.

I. For those to be ordained.

Almighty God, the giver of all good gifts, who of thy divine

providence hast appointed various orders in thy Church:

Give thy grace, we humbly beseech thee, to all who are [now]

called to any office and ministry for thy people; and so fill

them with the truth of thy doctrine and clothe them with

holiness of life, that they may faithfully serve before thee, to

the glory of thy great Name and for the benefit of thy holy

Church; through Jesus Christ our Lord, who liveth and

reigneth with thee, in the unity of the Holy Spirit, one God,

now and for ever. Amen.

Preface of Apostles

II. For the Choice of Fit Persons for the Ministry

O God, who didst lead thy holy apostles to ordain ministers

in every place: Grant that thy Church, under the guidance of

the Holy Spirit, may choose suitable persons for the ministry

of Word and Sacrament, and may uphold them in their work

for the extension of thy kingdom; through him who is the
Shepherd and Bishop of our souls, Jesus Christ our Lord,
who liveth and reigneth with thee and the same Spirit, one
God, for ever and ever. Amen.

Preface of the Season

III. For all Christians in Their Vocation

Almighty and everlasting God, by whose Spirit the whole
body of thy faithful people is governed and sanctified:
Receive our supplications and prayers, which we offer before
thee for all members of thy holy Church, that in their
vocation and ministry they may truly and godly serve thee;
through our Lord and Savior Jesus Christ, who liveth and
reigneth with thee, in the unity of the same Spirit, one God,
now and for ever. Amen.

Preface of Baptism, or of the Season

16. For the Mission of the Church

O God, who hast made of one blood all the peoples of the
earth, and didst send thy blessed Son to preach peace to those
who are far off and to those who are near: Grant that people
everywhere may seek after thee and find thee, bring the
nations into thy fold, pour out thy Spirit upon all flesh, and

hasten the coming of thy kingdom; through the same thy Son Jesus Christ our Lord, who liveth and reigneth with thee and the same Spirit, one God, now and for ever.

Amen.

Or this…

O God of all the nations of the earth: Remember the multitudes who have been created in thine image but have not known the redeeming work of our Savior Jesus Christ and grant that, by the prayers and labors of thy holy Church, they may be brought to know and worship thee as thou hast been revealed in thy Son; who liveth and reigneth with thee and the Holy Spirit, one God, for ever and ever. Amen.

Preface of the Season, or of Pentecost

17. For the Nation

Lord God Almighty, who hast made all peoples of the earth for thy glory, to serve thee in freedom and peace: Grant to the people of our country a zeal for justice and the strength of forbearance, that we may use our liberty in accordance with thy gracious will; through Jesus Christ our Lord, who liveth and reigneth with thee and the Holy Spirit, one God, for ever and ever. Amen.

Preface of Trinity Sunday

18. For Peace

O Almighty God, kindle, we beseech thee, in every heart the true love of peace, and guide with thy wisdom those who take counsel for the nations of the earth, that in tranquillity thy dominion may increase till the earth is filled with the knowledge of thy love; through Jesus Christ our Lord, who liveth and reigneth with thee, in the unity of the Holy Spirit, one God, now and for ever. Amen.

Preface of the Season

19. For Rogation Days

For use on the traditional days or at other times.

I. For fruitful seasons

Almighty God, Lord of heaven and earth: We humbly pray that thy gracious providence may give and preserve to our use the harvests of the land and of the seas, and may prosper all who labor to gather them, that we, who constantly receive good things from thy hand, may always give thee thanks; through Jesus Christ our Lord, who liveth and reigneth with thee and the Holy Spirit, one God, for ever and ever. Amen.

Preface of the Season

II. For Commerce and Industry

Almighty God, whose Son Jesus Christ in his earthly life
shared our toil and hallowed our labor: Be present with
thy people where they work; make those who carry on
the industries and commerce of this land responsive to thy
will; and give to us all a pride in what we do, and a just
return for our labor; through Jesus Christ our Lord, who
liveth and reigneth with thee, in the unity of the Holy Spirit,
one God, now and for ever. Amen.

Preface of the Season

III. For Stewardship of Creation

O merciful Creator, whose hand is open wide to satisfy the
needs of every living creature: Make us, we beseech thee,
ever thankful for thy loving providence; and grant that we,
remembering the account that we must one day give, may be
faithful stewards of thy bounty; through Jesus Christ our
Lord, who with thee and the Holy Spirit liveth and reigneth,
one God, for ever and ever. Amen.

Preface of the Season

20. For the Sick

Heavenly Father, giver of life and health: Comfort and

relieve thy sick servants, and give thy power of healing to
those who minister to their needs, that those (or N., or NN.)
for whom our prayers are offered may be strengthened in
their weakness and have confidence in thy loving care;
through Jesus Christ our Lord, who liveth and reigneth with
thee and the Holy Spirit, one God, now and for ever. Amen.
Preface of the Season

21. For Social Justice

Almighty God, who hast created us in thine own image:
Grant us grace fearlessly to contend against evil and to make
no peace with oppression; and, that we may reverently use
our freedom, help us to employ it in the maintenance of
justice in our communities and among the nations, to the
glory of thy holy Name; through Jesus Christ our Lord, who
liveth and reigneth with thee and the Holy Spirit, one God,
now and for ever. Amen.

Preface of the Season

22. For Social Service

O Lord our heavenly Father, whose blessed Son came not to
be ministered unto but to minister: Bless, we beseech thee, all
who, following in his steps, give themselves to the service of

others; that with wisdom, patience, and courage, they may minister in his name to the suffering, the friendless, and the needy; for the love of him who laid down his life for us, the same thy Son our Savior Jesus Christ, who liveth and reigneth with thee and the Holy Spirit, one God, for ever and ever. Amen.

Preface of the Season

23. For Education

Almighty God, the fountain of all wisdom: Enlighten by thy Holy Spirit those who teach and those who learn, that, rejoicing in the knowledge of thy truth, they may worship thee and serve thee from generation to generation; through Jesus Christ our Lord, who liveth and reigneth with thee and the same Spirit, one God, for ever and ever. Amen.

Preface of the Season

24. For Vocation in Daily Work

Almighty God our heavenly Father, who declarest thy glory and showest forth thy handiwork in the heavens and in the earth: Deliver us, we beseech thee, in our several occupations from the service of self alone, that we may do the work which thou givest us to do, in truth and beauty and for the common good; for the sake of him who came among us as one that serveth, thy Son Jesus Christ our Lord, who liveth and reigneth with thee and the Holy Spirit, one God, for ever and ever. Amen.

Preface of the Season

25. For Labor Day

Almighty God, who hast so linked our lives one with another that all we do affects, for good or ill, all other lives: So guide us in the work we do, that we may do it not for self alone, but for the common good; and, as we seek a proper return for our own labor, make us mindful of the rightful aspirations of other workers, and arouse our concern for those who are out of work; through Jesus Christ our Lord, who liveth and reigneth with thee and the Holy Spirit, one God, for ever and ever. Amen.

Preface of the Season

Additional Directions

If Banns are to be published, the following form is used.

I publish the Banns of Marriage between N.N. of _____ and N. N. of _____ . If any of you know just cause why *they may not be joined together in Holy Matrimony, you are bidden to declare it.*

This is the first (or second, or third) time of asking.

The Celebration and Blessing of a Marriage may be used with any authorized liturgy for the Holy Eucharist. This service then replaces the Ministry of the Word, and the Eucharist begins with the Offertory.

After the Declaration of Consent, if there is to be a giving in marriage, or presentation, the Celebrant asks, *Who gives (presents) this woman to be married to this man?* Or the following...

Who presents this woman and this man to be married to each other?

To either question, the appropriate answer is, *"I do."* If more than one person responds, they do so together.

For the Ministry of the Word it is fitting that the man and woman to be married remain where they may conveniently hear the reading of Scripture. They may approach the Altar, either for the exchange of vows, or for the Blessing of the Marriage.

It is appropriate that all remain standing until the conclusion of the Collect. Seating may be provided for the wedding party, so that all may be seated for the Lessons and the homily.

The Apostles' Creed may be recited after the Lessons, or after the homily, if here is one.

When desired, some other suitable symbol of the vows may be used in place of the ring.

At the Offertory, it is desirable that the bread and wine be presented to the ministers by the newly married persons. They may then remain before the Lord's Table and receive Holy Communion before other members of the congregation.

A Thanksgiving for the Birth or Adoption of a Child

As soon as convenient after the birth of a child, or after receiving a child by adoption, the parents, with other members of the family, should come to the church to be welcomed by the congregation and to give thanks to Almighty God. It is desirable that this take place at a Sunday service. In the Eucharist it may follow the Prayers of the People preceding the Offertory. At Morning or Evening Prayer it may take place before the close of the Office.

When desired, a briefer form of this service may be used, especially in the hospital or at home; in which case the Celebrant may begin with the Act of Thanksgiving, or with the prayer "O God, you have taught us."

A passage from Scripture may first be read. Either Luke 2:41-51, or Luke 18:15-17, is appropriate.

During the prayers, some parents may wish to express thanks in their own words.

At the proper time, the Celebrant invites the parents and other members of the family to present themselves before the Altar.

For the Birth of a Child

The Celebrant addresses the congregation in these or similar words.

Dear Friends: The birth of a child is a joyous and solemn

occasion in the life of a family. It is also an occasion for

rejoicing in the Christian community. I bid you, therefore,

to join N. [and N.] in giving thanks to Almighty God our

heavenly Father, the Lord of all life, for the gift of N. to be

their son (daughter) [and with N. (and NN.), for a new

brother (sister)]. Let us say together:

The service continues with one of the Psalms.

For an Adoption

The Celebrant addresses the congregation in these or similar words.

Dear Friends: It has pleased God our heavenly Father to answer the earnest prayers of N. [and N.], member(s) of this Christian family, for the gift of a child. I bid you join with them [and with N. (and NN.), who now has a new brother (sister)] in offering heartfelt thanks for the joyful and solemn responsibility which is theirs by the coming of N. to be a member of their family. But first, our friends wish us, here assembled, to witness the inauguration of this new relationship.

The Celebrant asks the parent or parents...

N. [and N.], *do you take this child for your own?*

Parent(s): *I do.*

Then if the child is old enough to answer, the Celebrant asks...

N., do you take this woman as your mother?

Child: *I do.*

Celebrant: *Do you take this man as your father?*

Child: *I do.*

Then the Celebrant, holding or taking the child by the hand, gives the child to the mother or father, saying...

As God has made us his children by adoption and grace, may you receive N. as your own son (daughter).

Then one or both parents say these or similar words.

May God, the Father of all, bless our child N., and us who

have given to him our family name, that we may live together

in love and affection; through Jesus Christ our Lord. Amen.

The Celebrant says...

Since it has pleased God to bestow upon N. [and N.] the gift of a child, let us now give thanks to him, and say together:

The Song of Mary

My soul proclaims the greatness of the Lord,

my spirit rejoices in God my Savior;

for he has looked with favor on his lowly servant.

From this day all generations will call me blessed:

the Almighty has done great things for me,

and holy is his Name.

He has mercy on those who fear him

in every generation.

He has shown the strength of his arm,

he has scattered the proud in their conceit.

He has cast down the mighty from their thrones,

and has lifted up the lowly.

He has filled the hungry with good things,

and the rich he has sent away empty.

He has come to the help of his servant Israel,

for he has remembered his promise of mercy,

The promise he made to our fathers,

to Abraham and his children for ever.

Glory to the Father, and to the Son, and to the Holy Spirit:

as it was in the beginning, is now, and will be for ever. Amen.

Or this...

Psalm 116

I love the Lord, because he has heard the voice of my

supplication;

because he has inclined his ear to me whenever I called

upon him.

Gracious is the Lord and righteous;

our God is full of compassion.

How shall I repay the Lord

for all the good things he has done for me?

I will lift up the cup of salvation

and call upon the Name of the Lord,

I will fulfill my vows to the Lord

in the presence of all his people,

In the courts of the Lord's house,

in the midst of you, O Jerusalem.

Hallelujah!

Glory to the Father, and to the Son, and to the Holy Spirit:

as it was in the beginning, is now, and will be for ever. Amen.

Or this...

Psalm 23

The Lord is my shepherd;

I shall not be in want.

He makes me lie down in green pastures

and leads me beside still waters.

He revives my soul

and guides me along right pathways for his Name's sake.

Though I walk through the valley of the shadow of death,

I shall fear no evil;

for you are with me;

your rod and your staff, they comfort me.

You spread a table before me in the presence of those

who trouble me;

you have anointed my head with oil,

and my cup is running over.

Surely your goodness and mercy shall follow me all the

days of my life,

and I will dwell in the house of the Lord for ever.

Glory to the Father, and to the Son, and to the Holy Spirit:

as it was in the beginning, is now, and will be for ever. Amen.

The Celebrant then says this prayer.

Let us pray.

O God, you have taught us through your blessed Son that whoever receives a little child in the name of Christ receives Christ himself: We give you thanks for the blessing you have bestowed upon this family in giving them a child. Confirm their joy by a lively sense of your presence with them, and give them calm strength and patient wisdom as they seek to bring this child to love all that is true and noble, just and pure, lovable and gracious, excellent and admirable, following the example of our Lord and Savior, Jesus Christ. Amen.

Prayers

The Celebrant may add one or more of the following prayers for a safe delivery.

O gracious God, we give you humble and hearty thanks that you have preserved through the pain and anxiety of childbirth your servant N., who desires now to offer you her praises and thanksgivings. Grant, most merciful Father, that by your help she may live faithfully according to your will in this life, and finally partake of everlasting glory in the life to come; through Jesus Christ our Lord. Amen.

For the Parents

Almighty God, giver of life and love, bless N. and N. Grant them wisdom and devotion in the ordering of their common life, that each may be to the other a strength in need, a counselor in perplexity, a comfort in sorrow, and a companion in joy. And so knit their wills together in your will and their spirits in your Spirit, that they may live together in love and peace all the days of their life; through Jesus Christ our Lord. Amen.

For a Child Not Yet Baptized

O eternal God, you have promised to be a father to a thousand generations of those who love and fear you: Bless this child and preserve his life; receive him and enable him to receive you, that through the Sacrament of Baptism he may become the child of God; through Jesus Christ our Lord. Amen.

For a Child Already Baptized

Into your hands, O God, we place your child N. Support him in his successes and in his failures, in his joys and in his sorrows. As he grows in age, may he grow in grace, and in the knowledge of his Savior Jesus Christ. Amen.

The Celebrant may then bless the family.

May God the Father, who by Baptism adopts us as his

children, grant you grace. Amen.

May God the Son, who sanctified a home at Nazareth, fill

you with love. Amen.

May God the Holy Spirit, who has made the Church one

family, keep you in peace. Amen.

The Peace May be Exchanged.

The Minister of the Congregation is directed to instruct the people, from time to time, about the duty of Christian parents to make prudent provision for the well-being of their families, and of all persons to make wills, while they are in health, arranging for the disposal of their temporal goods, not neglecting, if they are able, to leave bequests for religious and charitable uses.

Holy Baptism

A hymn, psalm, or anthem may be sung. The people standing, the Celebrant says:

Blessed be God: Father, Son, and Holy Spirit.

People And blessed be his kingdom, now and for ever. Amen.

In place of the above, from Easter Day through the Day of Pentecost

Celebrant Alleluia. Christ is risen.

People The Lord is risen indeed. Alleluia.

In Lent and on other penitential occasions

Celebrant Bless the Lord who forgives all our sins;

People His mercy endures for ever.

The Celebrant then continues

There is one Body and one Spirit;

People There is one hope in God's call to us;

Celebrant One Lord, one Faith, one Baptism;

People One God and Father of all.

Celebrant The Lord be with you.

People And also with you.

Celebrant Let us pray.

Confirmation

With forms for Reception and for the Reaffirmation of Baptismal Vows, a hymn, psalm, or anthem may be sung.

The people standing, the Celebrant says:

Blessed be God: Father, Son, and Holy Spirit.

People And blessed be his kingdom, now and forever. Amen.

In place of the above, from Easter Day through the Day of Pentecost.

Alleluia. Christ is risen.

People The Lord is risen indeed. Alleluia.

In Lent and on other penitential occasions

Celebrant Bless the Lord who forgives all our sins.

People His mercy endures for ever.

The Celebrant then continues

There is one Body and one Spirit;

People There is one hope in God's call to us;

Celebrant One Lord, one Faith, one Baptism;

People One God and Father of all.

Celebrant The Lord be with you.

People And also with you.

Celebrant Let us pray.

Concerning the Service-2

In the course of their Christian development, those baptized at an early age are expected, when they are ready and have been duly prepared, to make a mature public affirmation of their faith and commitment to the responsibilities of their Baptism and to receive the laying on of hands by the bishop.

Those baptized as adults, unless baptized with laying on of hands by a bishop, are also expected to make a public affirmation of their faith and commitment to the responsibilities of their Baptism in the presence of a bishop and to receive the laying on of hands.

When there is no Baptism, the rites of Confirmation, Reception, and the Reaffirmation of Baptismal Vows are administered in the following form.

If desired, the hymn Gloria in excelsis may be sung immediately after the opening versicles and before the salutation "The Lord be with you."

The Nicene Creed is not used at this service.

It is appropriate that the oblations of bread and wine be presented by persons newly confirmed.

Confirmation with Forms for Reception and for the Reaffirmation of Baptismal Vows

A hymn, psalm, or anthem may be sung.

The people standing, the Bishop says:

Blessed be God: Father, Son, and Holy Spirit.

People And blessed be his kingdom, now and for ever. Amen.

In place of the above, from Easter Day through the Day of Pentecost.

Alleluia. Christ is risen. People The Lord is risen indeed. Alleluia.

In Lent and on other penitential occasions

Bishop: Bless the Lord who forgives all our sins.

People: His mercy endures for ever.

The Bishop then continues

There is one Body and one Spirit;

People: There is one hope in God's call to us;

Bishop: One Lord, one Faith, one Baptism;

People: One God and Father of all.

Bishop: The Lord be with you.

People: And also with you.

Bishop: Let us pray.

People: Amen.

The people sit. One or two Lessons, as appointed, are read, the Reader first saying:

A Reading (Lesson) from ___(your choice)___ .

A citation giving chapter and verse may be added.

After each Reading the Reader may say

The Word of the Lord.

People: Thanks be to God.

or the Reader may say *Here ends the Reading (Epistle).*

Silence may follow.

A Psalm, hymn, or anthem may follow each Reading.

Then, all standing, the Deacon or a Priest reads the Gospel, first saying:

The Holy Gospel of our Lord Jesus Christ

according to _____ .

People Glory to you, Lord Christ.

After the Gospel, the Reader says

The Gospel of the Lord.

People Praise to you, Lord Christ.

The Sermon - Presentation and Examination of the Candidates

The Bishop says:

The Candidate(s) will now be presented.

Presenters I present these persons for Confirmation.

Or: I present these persons to be received into this Communion.

Or: *I present these persons who desire to reaffirm their baptismal vows.*

The Bishop asks the candidates:

Do you reaffirm your renunciation of evil?

Candidate: *I do.*

Bishop: *Do you renew your commitment to Jesus Christ?*

Candidate: *I do, and with God's grace I will follow him as my Savior and Lord.*

After all have been presented, the Bishop addresses the congregation, saying:

Will you who witness these vows do all in your power to support these persons in their life in Christ?

People: *We will.*

The Bishop then says these or similar words.

Let us join with those who are committing themselves to Christ and renew our own baptismal covenant.

The Baptismal Covenant

Bishop: *Do you believe in God the Father?*

People: *I believe in God, the Father almighty,*

creator of heaven and earth.

Bishop: *Do you believe in Jesus Christ, the Son of God?*

People: *I believe in Jesus Christ, his only Son, our Lord.*

He was conceived by the power of the Holy Spirit

and born of the Virgin Mary.

He suffered under Pontius Pilate,

was crucified, died, and was buried.

He descended to the dead.

On the third day he rose again.

He ascended into heaven,

and is seated at the right hand of the Father.

He will come again to judge the living and the dead.

Bishop: *Do you believe in God the Holy Spirit?*

People: *I believe in the Holy Spirit,*

the holy catholic Church,

the communion of saints,

the forgiveness of sins,

the resurrection of the body,

and the life everlasting.

Bishop: *Will you continue in the apostles' teaching and*

fellowship, in the breaking of bread, and in the prayers?

People: *I will, with God's help.*

Bishop: *Will you persevere in resisting evil, and, whenever you fall into sin, repent and return to the Lord?*

People: *I will, with God's help.*

Bishop: *Will you proclaim by word and example the Good News of God in Christ?*

People: *I will, with God's help.*

Bishop: *Will you seek and serve Christ in all persons, loving your neighbor as yourself?*

People: *I will, with God's help.*

Bishop: *Will you strive for justice and peace among all people, and respect the dignity of every human being?*

People: *I will, with God's help.*

Prayers for the Candidates

The Bishop then says to the congregation:

Let us now pray for these persons who have renewed their commitment to Christ.

Petitions may be used.

A period of silence follows.

Then the Bishop says:

Almighty God, we thank you that by the death and resurrection of your Son Jesus Christ you have overcome sin and brought us to yourself, and that by the sealing of your Holy Spirit you have bound us to your service. Renew in these your servants the covenant you made with them at their Baptism. Send them forth in the power of that Spirit to perform the service you set before them; through Jesus Christ your Son our Lord, who lives and reigns with you and the Holy Spirit, one God, now and for ever. Amen.

For Confirmation

The Bishop lays hands upon each one and says:

Strengthen, O Lord, your servant N. with your Holy Spirit;

empower him for your service; and sustain him all the days

of his life. Amen.

Or this:

Defend, O Lord, your servant N. with your heavenly grace,

that he may continue yours for ever, and daily increase in

your Holy Spirit more and more, until he comes to your

everlasting kingdom. Amen.

For Reception

N., we recognize you as a member of the one holy catholic

and apostolic Church, and we receive you into the fellowship

of this Communion. God, the Father, Son, and Holy Spirit,

bless, preserve, and keep you. Amen.

For Reaffirmation

N., may the Holy Spirit, who has begun a good work in you,

direct and uphold you in the service of Christ and his

kingdom. Amen.

The Bishop concludes with this prayer.

Almighty and everliving God, let your fatherly hand ever be over these your servants; let your Holy Spirit ever be with them; and so lead them in the knowledge and obedience of your Word, that they may serve you in this life, and dwell with you in the life to come; through Jesus Christ our Lord. Amen.

The Peace is then Exchanged

Bishop: *The peace of the Lord be always with you.*

People: *And also with you.*

The service then continues with the Prayers of the People or the Offertory of the Eucharist, at which the bishop should be the principal celebrant. If there is no celebration of the Eucharist, the service continues with the Lord's Prayer and such other devotions as the bishop may direct. The bishop may consecrate oil of Chrism for use at Baptism, using a prayer

A Form of Commitment to Christian Service

This form may be used when a person wishes to make or renew a Commitment to the service of Christ in the world, either in general terms, or upon undertaking some special responsibility. It is essential that the person seeking to make or renew a commitment prepare in advance, in consultation with the celebrant, the Act of Commitment, which may be in the form either of a statement of intention or of a series of questions and answers, but which should include a reaffirmation of baptismal promises.

Before the Offertory of the Eucharist, the person comes forward at the invitation of the celebrant, and, standing before the congregation, makes the Act of Commitment.

After this, the Celebrant says these or similar words:

May the Holy Spirit guide and strengthen you, that in this,

and in all things, you may do God's will in the service of the

kingdom of his Christ. Amen.

In the name of this congregation I commend you to this

work, and pledge you our prayers, encouragement, and

support.

The Celebrant then says this or some other appropriate prayer.

Let us pray.

Almighty God, look with favor upon this person who has

now reaffirmed his commitment to follow Christ and to serve

in his name. Give him courage, patience, and vision; and

strengthen us all in our Christian vocation of witness to the

world, and of service to others; through Jesus Christ our

Lord. Amen.

A prayer for the special work in which the person will be engaged may be added. The service then continues with the exchange of the Peace and the Offertory.

Christian Marriage Placement

(Bride and groom both facing minister)

Bride Stands Here   Groom stands Here

X   X

Minister Stands Here (facing bride and groom)

X

The Celebration and Blessing of a Marriage

At the time appointed, the persons to be married, with their witnesses, assemble in the church or some other appropriate place. During their entrance, a hymn, psalm, or anthem may be sung, or instrumental music may be played.

Then the Celebrant, facing the people and the persons to be married, with the woman to the right and the man to the left, addresses the congregation and says:

Dearly beloved: We have come together in the presence of

God to witness and bless the joining together of this man and

this woman in Holy Matrimony. The bond and covenant of

marriage was established by God in creation, and our Lord

Jesus Christ adorned this manner of life by his presence and

first miracle at a wedding in Cana of Galilee. It signifies to us

the mystery of the union between Christ and his Church, and

Holy Scripture commends it to be honored among all people.

The union of husband and wife in heart, body, and mind is intended by God for their mutual joy; for the help and comfort given one another in prosperity and adversity; and, when it is God's will, for the procreation of children and their nurture in the knowledge and love of the Lord. Therefore marriage is not to be entered into unadvisedly or lightly, but reverently, deliberately, and in accordance with the purposes for which it was instituted by God.

Into this holy union N.N. and N.N. now come to be joined. If any of you can show just cause why they may not lawfully be married, speak now; or else for ever hold your peace.

Then the Celebrant says to the persons to be married

I require and charge you both, here in the presence of God, that if either of you know any reason why you may not be united in marriage lawfully, and in accordance with God's Word, you do now confess it.

The Declaration of Consent

The Celebrant says to the woman:

N., will you have this man to be your husband; to live together in the covenant of marriage? Will you love him, comfort him, honor and keep him, in sickness and in health; and, forsaking all others, be faithful to him as long as you both shall live?

The Woman answers:

I will.

The Celebrant says to the man:

N., will you have this woman to be your wife; to live together in the covenant of marriage? Will you love her, comfort her, honor and keep her, in sickness and in health; and, forsaking all others, be faithful to her as long as you both shall live?

The Man answers:

I will.

The Celebrant then addresses the congregation, saying:

Will all of you witnessing these promises do all in your power to uphold these two persons in their marriage?

People: *We will.*

If there is to be a presentation or a giving in marriage, it takes place at this time.

A hymn, psalm, or anthem may follow.

The Ministry of the Word

The Celebrant then says to the people:

The Lord be with you.

People And also with you.

Let us pray.

O gracious and ever living God, you have created us male and female in your image: Look mercifully upon this man and this woman who come to you seeking your blessing, and assist them with your grace, that with true fidelity and steadfast love they may honor and keep the promises and vows they make; through Jesus Christ our Savior, who lives and reigns with you in the unity of the Holy Spirit, one God, for ever and ever.

Amen.

Then one or more of the following passages from Holy Scripture is read. If there is to be a Communion, a passage from the Gospel always concludes the Readings.

Genesis 1:26-28 (Male and female he created them)

Genesis 2:4-9, 15-24 (A man cleaves to his wife and they become one flesh)

Song of Solomon 2:10-13; 8:6-7 (Many waters cannot quench love)

Tobit 8:5b-8 (New English Bible) (That she and I may grow old together)

1 Corinthians 13:1-13 (Love is patient and kind)

Ephesians 3:14-19 (The Father from whom every family is named)

Ephesians 5:1-2, 21-33 (Walk in love, as Christ loved us)

Colossians 3:12-17 (Love which binds everything together in harmony)

1 John 4:7-16 (Let us love one another for love is of God)

Between the Readings, a Psalm, hymn, or anthem may be sung or said.

Appropriate Psalms are 67, 127, and 128.

When a passage from the Gospel is to be read, all stand, and the Deacon or Minister appointed says:

The Holy Gospel of our Lord Jesus Christ

according to _____ .

People: *Glory to you, Lord Christ.*

Matthew 5:1-10 (The Beatitudes)

Matthew 5:13-16 (You are the light . . . Let your light so shine)

Matthew 7:21, 24-29 (Like a wise man who built his house upon the rock)

Mark 10:6-9, 13-16 (They are no longer two but one)

John 15:9-12 (Love one another as I have loved you)

After the Gospel, the Reader says:

The Gospel of the Lord.

People Praise to you, Lord Christ.

A homily or other response to the Readings may follow.

The Marriage

The Man, facing the woman and taking her right hand in his, says:

In the Name of God, I, N., take you, N., to be my wife, to

have and to hold from this day forward, for better for worse,

for richer for poorer, in sickness and in health, to love and to

cherish, until we are parted by death. This is my solemn vow.

Then they loose their hands, and the Woman, still facing the man, takes his right hand in hers, and says

In the Name of God, I, N., take you, N., to be my husband,

to have and to hold from this day forward, for better for

worse, for richer for poorer, in sickness and in health, to love

and to cherish, until we are parted by death. This is my

solemn vow.

They loose their hands.

The Priest may ask God's blessing on a ring or rings as follows:

Bless, O Lord, this ring to be a sign of the vows by which

this man and this woman have bound themselves to each

other; through Jesus Christ our Lord. Amen.

The giver places the ring on the ring-finger of the other's hand and says:

N., I give you this ring as a symbol of my vow, and with all

that I am, and all that I have, I honor you, in the Name of

the Father, and of the Son, and of the Holy Spirit (or in the

Name of God).

Then the Celebrant joins the right hands of husband and wife and says:

Now that N. and N. have given themselves to each other by

solemn vows, with the joining of hands and the giving and

receiving of a ring, I pronounce that they are husband

and wife, in the Name of the Father, and of the Son, and

of the Holy Spirit.

Those whom God has joined together let no one put asunder.

People: *Amen.*

The Prayers

All standing, the Celebrant says:

Let us pray together in the words our Savior taught us.

People and Celebrant:

Our Father, who art in heaven, Our Father in heaven,

hallowed be thy Name, hallowed be your Name,

thy kingdom come, your kingdom come,

thy will be done, your will be done,

on earth as it is in heaven. On earth as it isinheaven.

Give us this day our daily bread. Give us today our daily bread.

And forgive us our trespasses, Forgive us our sins

as we forgive those us we forgive those

who trespass against us. who sin against us.

And lead us not into temptation, Save us from the time of trial,

but deliver us from evil. and deliver us from evil.

For thine is the kingdom, For the kingdom, the power,

and the power, and the glory, and the glory are yours,

for ever and ever. Amen. now and for ever. Amen.

If Communion is to follow, the Lord's Prayer may be omitted here.

The Celebrant or other person appointed reads the following prayers, to which the People respond, saying, Amen.

If there is not to be a Communion, one or more of the prayers may be omitted.

Let us pray.

Eternal God, creator and preserver of all life, author of

salvation, and giver of all grace: Look with favor upon the

world you have made, and for which your Son gave his life,

and especially upon this man and this woman whom you

make one flesh in Holy Matrimony. Amen.

Give them wisdom and devotion in the ordering of their

common life, that each may be to the other a strength in need, a

counselor in perplexity, a comfort in sorrow, and a companion

in joy. Amen.

Grant that their wills may be so knit together in your will,

and their spirits in your Spirit, that they may grow in love

and peace with you and one another all the days of their life.

Amen.

Give them grace, when they hurt each other, to recognize and

acknowledge their fault, and to seek each other's forgiveness

and yours. Amen.

Make their life together a sign of Christ's love to this sinful

and broken world, that unity may overcome estrangement,

forgiveness heal guilt, and joy conquer despair. Amen.

Bestow on them, if it is your will, the gift and heritage of

children, and the grace to bring them up to know you, to love

you, and to serve you. Amen.

Give them such fulfillment of their mutual affection that they

may reach out in love and concern for others. Amen.

Grant that all married persons who have witnessed these

vows may find their lives strengthened and their loyalties

confirmed. Amen.

Grant that the bonds of our common humanity, by which all

your children are united one to another, and the living to the

dead, may be so transformed by your grace, that your will may

be done on earth as it is in heaven; where, O Father, with your

Son and the Holy Spirit, you live and reign in perfect unity,

now and for ever. Amen.

The Blessing of the Marriage

The people remain standing. The husband and wife kneel, and the Priest says one of the following prayers:

Most gracious God, we give you thanks for your tender love

in sending Jesus Christ to come among us, to be born of a

human mother, and to make the way of the cross to be the

way of life. We thank you, also, for consecrating the union of man and woman in his Name. By the power of your Holy

Spirit, pour out the abundance of your blessing upon this

man and this woman. Defend them from every enemy. Lead

them into all peace. Let their love for each other be a seal

upon their hearts, a mantle about their shoulders, and a

crown upon their foreheads. Bless them in their work and in

their companionship; in their sleeping and in their waking; in

their joys and in their sorrows; in their life and in their death.

Finally, in your mercy, bring them to that table where your

saints feast for ever in your heavenly home; through Jesus

Christ our Lord, who with you and the Holy Spirit lives and

reigns, one God, for ever and ever. Amen.

Or this:

O God, you have so consecrated the covenant of marriage

that in it is represented the spiritual unity between Christ

and his Church: Send therefore your blessing upon these your

servants, that they may so love, honor, and cherish each other

in faithfulness and patience, in wisdom and true godliness,

that their home may be a haven of blessing and peace;

through Jesus Christ our Lord, who lives and reigns with you

and the Holy Spirit, one God, now and for ever. Amen.

The husband and wife still kneeling, the Priest adds this blessing

God the Father, God the Son, God the Holy Spirit, bless,

preserve, and keep you; the Lord mercifully with his favor

look upon you, and fill you with all spiritual benediction and

grace; that you may faithfully live together in this life, and

in the age to come have life everlasting. Amen.

The Peace

The Celebrant may say to the people:

The peace of the Lord be always with you.

People: *And also with you.*

The newly married couple then greets each other, after which greetings may be exchanged throughout the congregation.

When Communion is not to follow, the wedding party leaves the church. A hymn, psalm, or anthem may be sung, or instrumental music may be played.

The Blessing of a Civil Marriage

The Rite begins as prescribed for celebrations of the Holy Eucharist, using the Collect and Lessons appointed in the Marriage service. After the Gospel (and homily), the husband and wife stand before the Celebrant, who addresses them in these or similar words.

N. and N., you have come here today to seek the blessing of

God and of his Church upon your marriage. I require,

therefore, that you promise, with the help of God, to fulfill

the obligations which Christian Marriage demands.

The Celebrant then addresses the husband, saying:

N., you have taken N. to be your wife. Do you promise to love her, comfort her, honor and keep her, in sickness and in health; and, forsaking all others, to be faithful to her as long as you both shall live?

The Husband answers I do.

The Celebrant then addresses the wife, saying:

N., you have taken N. to be your husband. Do you promise to love him, comfort him, honor and keep him, in sickness and in health; and, forsaking all others, to be faithful to him as long as you both shall live?

The Wife answers I do.

Blessing of a Marriage

The Celebrant then addresses the congregation, saying:

Will you who have witnessed these promises do all in your power to uphold these two persons in their marriage?

People: *We will.*

If a ring or rings are to be blessed, the wife extends her hand (and the husband extends his hand) toward the Priest, who says:

Bless, O Lord, this ring to be a sign of the vows by which this man and this woman have bound themselves to each other; through Jesus Christ our Lord. Amen.

The Celebrant joins the right hands of the husband and wife and says:

Those whom God has joined together let no one put asunder.

The Congregation responds *Amen.*

An Order for Marriage

If it is desired to celebrate a marriage otherwise than as provided. Normally, the celebrant is a priest or bishop. When no priest or bishop is available, a deacon may function as celebrant, but does not pronounce a nuptial blessing. Or any religious clergy may officiate.

The laws of the State and the canons of this Church having been complied with, the man and the woman, together with their witnesses, families, and friends assemble in the church or in some other convenient place.

1. The teaching of the Church concerning Holy Matrimony, as it is declared in the formularies and canons of this Church, is briefly stated.

2. The intention of the man and the woman to enter the state of matrimony, and their free consent, is publicly ascertained.

3. One or more Readings, one of which is always from Holy Scripture, may precede the exchange of vows. If there is to be a Communion, a Reading from the Gospel is always included.

4. The vows of the man and woman are exchanged, using the following form:

In the Name of God, I, N., take you, N., to be my

(wife) (husband), to have and to hold from this day forward,

for better, for worse, for richer for poorer, in sickness and in

health, to love and to cherish, until we are parted by death.

This is my solemn vow.

Or this:

I, N., take thee N., to my wedded (wife) (husband), to have

and to hold from this day forward, for better for worse, for

richer for poorer, in sickness and in health, to love and to

cherish, till death us do part, according to God's holy

ordinance; and thereto I (plight) (give) thee my troth.

5. The Celebrant declares the union of the man and woman as husband and wife, in the Name of the Father, and of the Son, and of the Holy Spirit.

6. Prayers are offered for the husband and wife, for their life together, for the Christian community, and for the world.

7. A priest or bishop pronounces a solemn blessing upon the couple.

8. If there is no Communion, the service concludes with the Peace, the husband and wife first greeting each other. The Peace may be exchanged throughout the assembly.

9. If there is to be a Communion, the service continues with the Peace and the Offertory. The Holy Eucharist may be celebrated

Ministration at the Time of Death

When a person is near death, the Minister of the Congregation should be notified, in order that the ministrations of the Church may be provided.

A Prayer for a Person Near Death

Almighty God, look on this your servant, lying in great

weakness, and comfort him with the promise of life

everlasting, given in the resurrection of your Son Jesus

Christ our Lord. Amen.

<u>Litany at the Time of Death</u>

When possible, it is desirable that members of the family and friends come together to join in the Litany.

God the Father,

Have mercy on your servant.

God the Son,

Have mercy on your servant.

God the Holy Spirit,

Have mercy on your servant.

Holy Trinity, one God,

Have mercy on your servant.

From all evil, from all sin, from all tribulation,

Good Lord, deliver him.

By your holy Incarnation, by your Cross and Passion, by your precious Death and Burial,

Good Lord, deliver him.

By your glorious Resurrection and Ascension, and by the Coming of the Holy Spirit,

Good Lord, deliver him.

We sinners beseech you to hear us, Lord Christ: That it may please you to deliver the soul of your servant from the power

of evil, and from eternal death,

We beseech you to hear us, good Lord.

That it may please you mercifully to pardon all his sins,

We beseech you to hear us, good Lord.

That it may please you to grant him a place of refreshment

and everlasting blessedness,

We beseech you to hear us, good Lord.

That it may please you to give him joy and gladness in your

kingdom, with your saints in light,

We beseech you to hear us, good Lord.

Jesus, Lamb of God:

Have mercy on him.

Jesus, bearer of our sins:

Have mercy on him.

Jesus, redeemer of the world:

Give him your peace.

Lord, have mercy.

Christ, have mercy.

Lord, have mercy.

Celebrant and People

Our Father, who art in heaven, Our Father in heaven,

hallowed be thy Name, hallowed be your Name,

thy kingdom come, your kingdom come,

thy will be done, your will be done,

on earth as it is in heaven. on earth as in heaven.

Give us this day our daily bread. Give us today our daily bread.

And forgive us our trespasses, Forgive us our sins

as we forgive those as we forgive those

who trespass against us. who sin against us.

And lead us not into temptation, Save us from the time of trial,

but deliver us from evil. and deliver us from evil.

The Celebrant says this Collect

Let us pray.

Deliver your servant, N., O Sovereign Lord Christ, from all

evil, and set him free from every bond; that he may rest with

all your saints in the eternal habitations; where with the

Father and the Holy Spirit you live and reign, one God, for

ever and ever. Amen.

A Commendation at the Time of Death

Depart, O Christian soul, out of this world;

In the name of God the Father Almighty who created you;

In the name of Jesus Christ who redeemed you;

In the name of the Holy Spirit who sanctifies you.

May your rest be this day in peace,

and your dwelling place in the Paradise of God.

A Commendatory Prayer

Into your hands, O merciful Savior, we commend your

servant N. Acknowledge, we humbly beseech you, a sheep of

your own fold, a lamb of your own flock, a sinner of your

own redeeming. Receive him into the arms of your mercy,

into the blessed rest of everlasting peace, and into the

glorious company of the saints in light. Amen.

May his soul and the souls of all the departed, through the

mercy of God, rest in peace. Amen.

ask through Christ our Lord. Amen.

The Burial of the Dead: Rite

All stand while one or more of the following anthems are sung or said. A hymn, psalm, or some other suitable anthem may be sung instead.

I am Resurrection and I am Life, says the Lord.

Whoever has faith in me shall have life,

even though he die.

And everyone who has life,

and has committed himself to me in faith,

shall not die for ever.

As for me, I know that my Redeemer lives

and that at the last he will stand upon the earth.

After my awaking, he will raise me up;

and in my body I shall see God.

I myself shall see, and my eyes behold him

who is my friend and not a stranger.

For none of us has life in himself,

and none becomes his own master when he dies.

For if we have life, we are alive in the Lord,

and if we die, we die in the Lord.

So, then, whether we live or die,

we are the Lord's possession.

Happy from now on

are those who die in the Lord!

So it is, says the Spirit,

for they rest from their labors.

Or else this anthem:

In the midst of life we are in death;

from whom can we seek help?

From you alone, O Lord,

who by our sins are justly angered.

Holy God, Holy and Mighty,

Holy and merciful Savior,

deliver us not into the bitterness of eternal death.

Lord, you know the secrets of our hearts;

shut not your ears to our prayers,

but spare us, O Lord.

Holy God, Holy and Mighty,

Holy and merciful Savior,

deliver us not into the bitterness of eternal death.

O worthy and eternal Judge,

do not let the pains of death

turn us away from you at our last hour.

Holy God, Holy and Mighty,

Holy and merciful Savior,

deliver us not into the bitterness of eternal death.

When all are in place, the Celebrant may address the congregation,

acknowledging briefly the purpose of their gathering, and bidding their

prayers for the deceased and the bereaved.

The Celebrant then says: *The Lord be with you.*

People: *And also with you.*

Celebrant: *Let us pray.*

Silence may be kept; after which the Celebrant says one of the following:

At the Burial of an Adult

O God, who by the glorious resurrection of your Son Jesus

Christ destroyed death, and brought life and immortality to light: Grant that your servant N., being raised with him, may know the strength of his presence, and rejoice in his eternal glory; who with you and the Holy Spirit lives and reigns, one God, for ever and ever. Amen.

Or this:

O God, whose mercies cannot be numbered: Accept our prayers on behalf of your servant N., and grant him an entrance into the land of light and joy, in the fellowship of your saints; through Jesus Christ our Lord, who lives and reigns with you and the Holy Spirit, one God, now and for ever. Amen.

Or this:

O God of grace and glory, we remember before you this day our brother (sister) N. We thank you for giving him to us, his family and friends, to know and to love as a companion on our earthly pilgrimage. In your boundless compassion, console us who mourn. Give us faith to see in death the gate of eternal life, so that in quiet confidence we may continue our course on earth, until, by your call, we are reunited with those who have gone before; through Jesus Christ our Lord. Amen.

At the Burial of a Child

O God, whose beloved Son took children into his arms and blessed them: Give us grace to entrust N., to your never failing care and love, and bring us all to your heavenly kingdom; through Jesus Christ our Lord, who lives and reigns with you and the Holy Spirit, one God, now and for ever. Amen.

The Celebrant may add the following prayer:

Most merciful God, whose wisdom is beyond our understanding, deal graciously with NN. in their grief. Surround them with your love, that they may not be overwhelmed by their loss, but have confidence in your goodness, and strength to meet the days to come; through Jesus Christ our Lord. Amen.

The people sit.

One or more of the following passages from Holy Scripture is read. If there is to be a Communion, a passage from the Gospel always concludes the Readings.

The Liturgy of the Word

From the Old Testament:

Isaiah 25:6-9 (He will swallow up death for ever)

Isaiah 61:1-3 (To comfort those who mourn)

Lamentations 3:22-26, 31-33 (The Lord is good to those who wait for him)

Wisdom 3:1-5, 9 (The souls of the righteous are in the hands of God)

Job 19:21-27a (I know that my Redeemer lives)

A suitable psalm, hymn, or canticle may follow. The following Psalms are appropriate: 42:1-7, 46, 90:1-12, 121, 130, 139:1-11.

From the New Testament:

Romans 8:14-19, 34-35, 37-39 (The glory that shall be revealed)

1 Corinthians 15:20-26, 35-38, 42-44, 53-58 (The imperishable body)

2 Corinthians 4:16––5:9 (Things that are unseen are eternal)

1 John 3:1-2 (We shall be like him)

Revelation 7:9-17 (God will wipe away every tear)

Revelation 21:2-7 (Behold, I make all things new)

A suitable psalm, hymn, or canticle may follow. The following Psalms are appropriate: 23, 27, 106:1-5, 116.

The Gospel:

Then, all standing, the Deacon or Minister appointed reads the Gospel, first saying: *The Holy Gospel of our Lord Jesus Christ according to John.*

People: *Glory to you, Lord Christ.*

John 5:24-27 (He who believes has everlasting life)

John 6:37-40 (All that the Father gives me will come to me)

John 10:11-16 (I am the good shepherd)

John 11:21-27 (I am the resurrection and the life)

John 14:1-6 (In my Father's house are many rooms)

At the end of the Gospel, the Reader says: *The Gospel of the Lord.*

People: *Praise to you, Lord Christ.*

Here there may be a homily by the Celebrant, or a member of the family, or a friend.

The Apostles' Creed may then be said, all standing. The Celebrant may introduce the Creed with these or similar words:

In the assurance of eternal life given at Baptism, let us

proclaim our faith and say,

Celebrant and People:

I believe in God, the Father almighty,

creator of heaven and earth.

I believe in Jesus Christ, his only Son, our Lord.

He was conceived by the power of the Holy Spirit

and born of the Virgin Mary.

He suffered under Pontius Pilate,

was crucified, died, and was buried.

He descended to the dead.

On the third day he rose again.

He ascended into heaven,

and is seated at the right hand of the Father.

He will come again to judge the living and the dead.

I believe in the Holy Spirit,

the holy catholic Church,

the communion of saints,

the forgiveness of sins,

the resurrection of the body,

and the life everlasting. Amen.

If there is not to be a Communion, the Lord's Prayer is said here, and the service continues with the Prayers of the People. When there is a Communion, the following form of the Prayers of the People is used

For our brother (sister) N., let us pray to our Lord Jesus

Christ who said," I am Resurrection and I am Life."

Lord, you consoled Martha and Mary in their distress; draw

near to us who mourn for N., and dry the tears of those who

weep.

Hear us, Lord.

You wept at the grave of Lazarus, your friend; comfort us in

our sorrow.

Hear us, Lord.

You raised the dead to life; give to our brother (sister) eternal

life.

Hear us, Lord.

You promised paradise to the thief who repented; bring our

brother (sister) to the joys of heaven.

Hear us, Lord.

Our brother (sister) was washed in Baptism and anointed

with the Holy Spirit; give him fellowship with all your saints.

Hear us, Lord.

He was nourished with your Body and Blood; grant him a

place at the table in your heavenly kingdom.

Hear us, Lord.

Comfort us in our sorrows at the death of our brother

(sister); let our faith be our consolation, and eternal life our

hope.

Silence may be kept.

The Celebrant concludes with one of the following or some other prayer:

Lord Jesus Christ, we commend to you our brother (sister)

N., who was reborn by water and the Spirit in Holy Baptism.

Grant that his death may recall to us your victory over death,

and be an occasion for us to renew our trust in your Father's

love. Give us, we pray, the faith to follow where you have led

the way; and where you live and reign with the Father and

the Holy Spirit, to the ages of ages. Amen.

Or this:

Father of all, we pray to you for N., and for all those whom

we love but see no longer. Grant to them eternal rest. Let

light perpetual shine upon them. May his soul and the souls of all the departed, through the mercy of God, rest in peace.

Amen.

When there is no Communion, the service continues with the **Commendation, or with the Committal.**

At the Eucharist. The service continues with the Peace and the Offertory.

Preface of the Commemoration of the Dead

In place of the usual post communion prayer, the following is said:

Almighty God, we thank you that in your great love you have

fed us with the spiritual food and drink of the Body and

Blood of your Son Jesus Christ, and have given us a foretaste

of your heavenly banquet. Grant that this Sacrament may be

to us a comfort in affliction, and a pledge of our inheritance

in that kingdom where there is no death, neither sorrow nor

crying, but the fullness of joy with all your saints; through

Jesus Christ our Savior. Amen.

If the body is not present, the service continues with the (blessing and) dismissal. Unless the Committal follows immediately in the church, the following Commendation is used.

The Commendation

The Celebrant and other ministers take their places at the body.

This anthem, or some other suitable anthem, or a hymn, may be sung or said:

Give rest, O Christ, to your servant(s) with your saints,

where sorrow and pain are no more,

neither sighing, but life everlasting.

You only are immortal, the creator and maker of mankind;

and we are mortal, formed of the earth, and to earth shall we

return. For so did you ordain when you created me, saying,

"You are dust, and to dust you shall return." All of us go down

to the dust; yet even at the grave we make our song: Alleluia,

alleluia, alleluia.

Give rest, O Christ, to your servant(s) with your saints,

where sorrow and pain are no more,

neither sighing, but life everlasting.

The Celebrant, facing the body, says:

Into your hands, O merciful Savior, we commend your

servant N. Acknowledge, we humbly beseech you, a sheep of

your own fold, a lamb of your own flock, a sinner of your

own redeeming. Receive him into the arms of your mercy,

into the blessed rest of everlasting peace, and into the

glorious company of the saints in light. Amen.

The Celebrant, or the Bishop if present, may then bless the people, and a Deacon or other Minister may dismiss them, saying:

Let us go forth in the name of Christ.

Thanks be to God.

As the body is borne from the church, a hymn, or one or more of these anthems may be sung or said:

Christ is risen from the dead, trampling down death by death,

and giving life to those in the tomb.

The Sun of Righteousness is gloriously risen, giving light to

those who sat in darkness and in the shadow of death.

The Lord will guide our feet into the way of peace, having

taken away the sin of the world.

Christ will open the kingdom of heaven to all who believe in

his Name, saying, Come, O blessed of my Father; inherit the

kingdom prepared for you.

Into paradise may the angels lead you. At your coming may

the martyrs receive you, and bring you into the holy city

Jerusalem.

Or one of these Canticles: The Song of Zechariah, The Song of Simeon, Christ our Passover

The Committal

The following anthem is sung or said:

Everyone the Father gives to me will come to me;

I will never turn away anyone who believes in me.

He who raised Jesus Christ from the dead

will also give new life to our mortal bodies

through his indwelling Spirit.

My heart, therefore, is glad, and my spirit rejoices;

my body also shall rest in hope.

You will show me the path of life;

in your presence there is fullness of joy,

and in your right hand are pleasures for evermore.

Then, while earth is cast upon the coffin, the Celebrant says these words:

In sure and certain hope of the resurrection to eternal life

through our Lord Jesus Christ, we commend to Almighty

*God our brother N., and we commit his body to the ground; ***

earth to earth, ashes to ashes, dust to dust. The Lord bless

him and keep him, the Lord make his face to shine upon him

and be gracious to him, the Lord lift up his countenance upon

him and give him peace. Amen.

* Or the deep, or the elements, or its resting place.

The Celebrant says:

The Lord be with you.

People And also with you.

Celebrant: *Let us pray.*

Celebrant and People:

Our Father, who art in heaven, Our Father in heaven,

hallowed be thy Name, hallowed be your Name,

thy kingdom come, your kingdom come,

thy will be done, your will be done,

on earth as it is in heaven. on earth as in heaven.

Give us this day our daily bread. Give us today our daily bread.

And forgive us our trespasses, Forgive us our sins

as we forgive those as we forgive those

who trespass against us. who sin against us.

And lead us not into temptation, Save us from the time of trial,

but deliver us from evil. and deliver us from evil.

For thine is the kingdom, For the kingdom, the power,

and the power, and the glory, and the glory are yours,

for ever and ever. Amen. now and for ever. Amen.

Other prayers may be added.

Then may be said:

Rest eternal grant to him, O Lord;

And let light perpetual shine upon him.

May his soul, and the souls of all the departed,

through the mercy of God, rest in peace. Amen.

The Celebrant dismisses the people with these words

Alleluia. Christ is risen.

People The Lord is risen indeed. Alleluia.

Celebrant: *Let us go forth in the name of Christ.*

People: *Thanks be to God.*

Or with the following:

The God of peace, who brought again from the dead our

Lord Jesus Christ, the great Shepherd of the sheep, through

the blood of the everlasting covenant: Make you perfect in

every good work to do his will, working in you that which is

well-pleasing in his sight; through Jesus Christ, to whom be

glory for ever and ever. Amen.

The Consecration of a Grave

If the grave is in a place that has not previously been set apart for Christian burial, the Priest may use the following prayer, either before the service of Committal or at some other convenient time.

O God, whose blessed Son was laid in a sepulcher in the

garden: Bless, we pray, this grave, and grant that he whose

body is (is to be) buried here may dwell with Christ in

paradise, and may come to your heavenly kingdom; through

your Son Jesus Christ our Lord. Amen.

Additional Prayers

Almighty God, with whom still live the spirits of those who die in the Lord, and with whom the souls of the faithful are in joy and felicity: We give you heartfelt thanks for the good examples of all your servants, who, having finished their course in faith, now find rest and refreshment. May we, with all who have died in the true faith of your holy Name, have perfect fulfillment and bliss in your eternal and everlasting glory, through Jesus Christ our Lord. Amen.

•　•　•

O God, whose days are without end, and whose mercies cannot be numbered: Make us, we pray, deeply aware of the shortness and uncertainty of human life; and let your Holy Spirit lead us in holiness and righteousness all our days; that, when we shall have served you in our generation, we may be gathered to our ancestors, having the testimony of a good conscience, in the communion of the Catholic Church, in the confidence of a certain faith, in the comfort of a religious and holy hope, in favor with you, our God, and in perfect charity with the world. All this we ask through Jesus Christ our Lord. Amen.

O God, the King of saints, we praise and glorify your holy
Name for all your servants who have finished their course in
your faith and fear: for the blessed Virgin Mary; for the holy
patriarchs, prophets, apostles, and martyrs; and for all your
other righteous servants, known to us and unknown; and we
pray that, encouraged by their examples, aided by their
prayers, and strengthened by their fellowship, we also may
be partakers of the inheritance of the saints in light; through
the merits of your Son Jesus Christ our Lord. Amen.

•　　•　　•

Lord Jesus Christ, by your death you took away the sting of
death: Grant to us your servants so to follow in faith where
you have led the way, that we may at length fall asleep
peacefully in you and wake up in your likeness; for your
tender mercies' sake. Amen.

•　　•　　•

Father of all, we pray to you for those we love, but see no
longer: Grant them your peace; let light perpetual shine upon
them; and, in your loving wisdom and almighty power, work
in them the good purpose of your perfect will; through Jesus
Christ our Lord. Amen.

Merciful God, Father of our Lord Jesus Christ who is the Resurrection and the Life: Raise us, we humbly pray, from the death of sin to the life of righteousness; that when we depart this life we may rest in him, and at the resurrection receive that blessing which your well-beloved Son shall then pronounce: "Come, you blessed of my Father, receive the kingdom prepared for you from the beginning of the world." Grant this, O merciful Father, through Jesus Christ, our Mediator and Redeemer. Amen.

· · ·

Grant, O Lord, to all who are bereaved the spirit of faith and courage, that they may have strength to meet the days to come with steadfastness and patience; not sorrowing as those without hope, but in thankful remembrance of your great goodness, and in the joyful expectation of eternal life with those they love. And this we ask in the Name of Jesus Christ our Savior. Amen.

· · ·

Almighty God, Father of mercies and giver of comfort: Deal graciously, we pray, with all who mourn; that, casting all their care on you, they may know the consolation of your love; through Jesus Christ our Lord. Amen.

An Order for Burial

When, for pastoral considerations, the burial rites in this book is deemed appropriate, the following form is used.

1. The body is received. The celebrant may meet the body and conduct it into the church or chapel, or it may be in place before the congregation assembles.

2. Anthems from Holy Scripture or psalms may be sung or said, or a hymn may be sung.

3. Prayer may be offered for the bereaved.

4. One or more passages of Holy Scripture are read. Psalms, hymns, or anthems may follow the readings. If there is to be a Communion, the last reading is from the Gospel.

5. A homily may follow the Readings, and the Apostles' Creed may be recited.

6. Prayer, including the Lord's Prayer, is offered for the deceased, for those who mourn, and for the Christian community, remembering the promises of God in Christ about eternal life.

7. The deceased is commended to God, and the body is committed to its resting place. The committal may take place either where the preceding service has been held, or at the graveside.

8. If there is a Communion, it precedes the commendation, and begins with the Peace and Offertory of the Eucharist. Any of the authorized Eucharistic prayers may be used.

Note:

The liturgy for the dead is an Easter liturgy. It finds all its meaning in the resurrection. Because Jesus was raised from the dead, we, too, shall be raised. The liturgy, therefore, is characterized by joy, in the certainty that "neither death, nor life, nor angels, nor principalities, nor things present, nor things to come, nor powers, nor height, nor depth, nor anything else in all creation, will be able to separate us from the love of God in Christ Jesus our Lord."

This joy, however, does not make human grief unchristian. The very love we have for each other in Christ brings deep sorrow when we are parted by death. Jesus himself wept at the grave of his friend. So, while we rejoice that one we love has entered into the nearer presence of our Lord, we sorrow in sympathy with those who mourn.

CONCLUSION

*** Remember, these are your basics but you can readjust them.

<u>Example of adjusting a marriage ceremony:</u>

Ceremony Written by the Couple:

A one ring ceremony, minister says:

Marriage is an act of Faith and a personal commitment. It is the blending of the love of two souls. Marriage should be a harmonious relationship that will be strengthened each day to last forever.

(His name), (Her name) offers you her love and trust so they will be safe with you. Do you take (Her name) to be your wedded wife, to love, to cherish for the rest of your life?

He says- **I do**.

(Her name), (His name) offers you his love and trust so they will be safe with you. Do you take (His name) to be your wedded husband, to love, to cherish for the rest of your life?

She says- **I do**.

Minister- *The ring please* (best man gives ring to groom). *May this ring be Blessed as the symbol of this union. May their home together be a loving sanctuary.*

(His name), please place the ring on (her name) finger (Groom puts ring on Her finger.) In placing this ring on (His name) finger, I, as an ordained minister, now pronounce you husband and wife. You may kiss the bride.

*** Go forth and minister in the way you were "called "to service. ***

<u>YES YOU CAN !!!</u>

If you enjoyed this book, please write us for our
<u>FREE catalog</u>.

Global Communications

P.O. Box 753

New Brunswick, NJ 08903

Email: <u>mrufo8@hotmail.com</u>

www.conspiracyjournal.com

MARIA WOULD LIKE TO SPEAK PERSONALLY WITH YOU!

CONTACT MARIA D' ANDREA FOR. . .

READINGS
Private by Phone/Mail/In Person

*

WORKSHOPS

*

SEMINARS

*

BOOKS AND PRODUCTS

*

MAIL ORDER COURSES

Contact Maria D'Andrea at:

Mailing address:
PO BOX 52
Mineola, NY 11501
Offices on Long Island and Manhattan

Phone: (631) 559-1248

Email: maria@mariadandrea.com

PayPal: mdandrea100@gmail.com

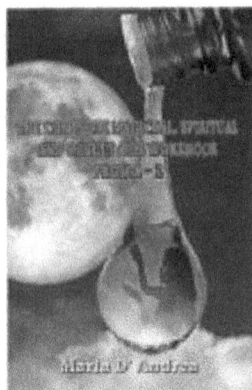

121

www.ingramcontent.com/pod-product-compliance
Lightning Source LLC
Chambersburg PA
CBHW081542040426
42448CB00015B/3187